THE BELOVED Psalms

JOURNAL

BELLE CITY GIFTS
SAVAGE, MINNESOTA, USA

BELLE CITY GIFTS IS AN IMPRINT OF BROADSTREET PUBLISHING GROUP, LLC.
BROADSTREETPUBLISHING.COM

PSALMS JOURNAL
© 2020 BY BROADSTREET PUBLISHING®

978-1-4245-6050-9

DESIGN BY CHRIS GARBORG | GARBORGDESIGN.COM
EDITORIAL SERVICES BY MICHELLE WINGER | LITERALLYPRECISE.COM

PRINTED IN CHINA.

20   21   22   23   24   25   26   7   6   5   4   3   2   1

Show me the right path, O Lord;
point out the road for me to follow.

PSALM 25:4 NLT

My heart has heard you say, "Come and talk with me."
And my heart responds, "LORD, I am coming."

PSALM 27:8 NLT

Honor the LORD for the glory of his name.
Worship the LORD in the splendor of his holiness.

PSALM 29:2 NLT

You have turned my mourning into joyful dancing.

PSALM 30:11 NLT

Oh, what joy for those whose disobedience is forgiven,
whose sin is put out of sight!

PSALM 32:1 NLT

Many are the sorrows of the wicked,
but steadfast love surrounds the one who trusts in the LORD.

PSALM 32:10 ESV

He loves righteousness and justice;
the earth is full of the steadfast love of the LORD.

PSALM 33:5 ESV

The plans of the LORD stand firm forever,
the purposes of his heart through all generations.

PSALM 33:11 NIV

Trust in the LORD, and do good;
dwell in the land and befriend faithfulness.

PSALM 37:3 ESV

There's no doubt about it;
God holds our lives safely in his hands.

PSALM 66: 9 TPT

Help him judge your people in the right way;
let the poor always be treated fairly.

PSALM 72:2 NLT

Father to the fatherless, defender of widows—
this is God, whose dwelling is holy.

PSALM 68:5 NLT

You rule the raging of the sea;
when its waves rise, you still them.

PSALM 89:9 ESV

I will be strength to him and I will give him my grace
to sustain him no matter what comes.

PSALM 89:21 TPT

Praise the LORD! Sing to the LORD a new song.
Sing his praises in the assembly of the faithful.

PSALM 149:1 NLT

Let all that I am praise the LORD;
may I never forget the good things he does for me.

PSALM 103:2 NLT

He redeems me from death
and crowns me with love and tender mercies.

PSALM 103:4 NLT

Cleanse me with hyssop, and I will be clean;
wash me, and I will be whiter than snow.

PSALM 51:7 NIV

Restore to me the joy of your salvation
and grant me a willing spirit, to sustain me.

PSALM 51:12 NIV

Let all who take refuge in you be glad;
let them ever sing for joy.

PSALM 5:11 NIV

Be strong, and let your heart take courage,
all you who wait for the LORD!

PSALM 31:24 ESV

He has not despised or scorned the suffering of the afflicted one;
he has not hidden his face from him but has listened to his cry for help.

PSALM 22:24 NIV

Know that the LORD has set apart his faithful servant for himself;
the LORD hears when I call to him.

You are enthroned as the Holy One;
you are the one Israel praises.

PSALM 22:3 NIV

In his hand are the depths of the earth,
and the mountain peaks belong to him.

PSALM 95:4 NIV

The LORD looks down from heaven on all mankind
to see if there are any who understand, any who seek God.

PSALM 14:2 NIV

I will bless the LORD who has counseled me;
indeed, my mind instructs me in the night.

PSALM 16:7 NASB

The word of the LORD is right and true;
he is faithful in all he does.

PSALM 33:4 NIV

Turn from evil and do good;
seek peace and pursue it.

PSALM 34:14 NIV

O God, you are my God; earnestly I seek you;
my soul thirsts for you; my flesh faints for you.

PSALM 63:1 ESV

May he grant you your heart's desire
and fulfill all your plans.

PSALM 20:4 ESV

Oh, that my actions would consistently reflect your decrees!

PSALM 119:5 NLT

How good and pleasant it is when God's people live together in unity!

PSALM 133:1 NIV

You are the fountain of life,
the light by which we see.

PSALM 36:9 NLT

Your goodness is as high as the mountains.
Your justice is as deep as the great ocean.

PSALM 36:6 NCV

Don't worry about the wicked
or envy those who do wrong.

PSALM 37:1 NLT

He will bring forth your righteousness as the light,
and your justice as the noonday.

PSALM 37:6 ESV

I lie down and sleep;
I wake again, because the LORD sustains me.

PSALM 3:3-4 NIV

The LORD also will be a refuge for the oppressed,
a refuge in times of trouble.

PSALM 9:9 NKJV

I call to you, God, and you answer me.
Listen to me now, and hear what I say.

PSALM 17:6 NCV

The LORD rules over the floodwaters.
The LORD reigns as king forever.

PSALM 29:10 NLT

I will extol the LORD at all times;
his praise will always be on my lips.

PSALM 34:1 NIV

For God alone, O my soul, wait in silence,
for my hope is from him.

PSALM 62:5 ESV

Bend down, O LORD, and hear my prayer;
answer me, for I need your help.

PSALM 86:1 NLT

You are near, O LORD,
and all your commands are true.

All he does is just and good,
and all his commandments are trustworthy.

PSALM 111:7 NLT

He provided redemption for his people;
he ordained his covenant forever—holy and awesome is his name.

PSALM 111:9 NIV

The fear of the LORD is the beginning of wisdom;
all those who practice it have a good understanding.

PSALM 111:10 ESV

Enter his gates with thanksgiving, and his courts with praise!
Give thanks to him; bless his name!

PSALM 100:4 ESV

Blessed be the LORD, the God of Israel,
From everlasting to everlasting.

PSALM 41:13 NASB

He satisfies me with good things
and makes me young again, like the eagle.

PSALM 103:5 NCV

O LORD, how manifold are your works!
In wisdom you have made them all.

PSALM 102:24 NRSV

He makes springs pour water into the ravines;
it flows between the mountains.

Not to us, LORD, not to us but to your name be the glory,
because of your love and faithfulness.

PSALM 115:1 NIV

Delight yourself in the LORD,
and he will give you the desires of your heart.

PSALM 37:4 ESV

I desire to do your will, my God;
your law is within my heart.

PSALM 40:8 NIV

O Lord, my Lord, the strength of my salvation,
you have covered my head in the day of battle.

PSALM 140:7 ESV

Like trees planted in the Temple of the LORD,
they will grow strong in the courtyards of our God.

PSALM 92:13 NCV

Fill us with your love every morning.
Then we will sing and rejoice all our lives.

PSALM 90:14 NCV

Let everything that has breath praise the LORD.
Praise the LORD.

PSALM 150:6 NIV

Let those who worship him rejoice in his glory.
Let them sing for joy even in bed!

PSALM 149:5 NCV

You open your hand;
you satisfy the desire of every living thing.

PSALM 145:16 ESV

He leads the humble in what is right,
and teaches the humble his way.

PSALM 25:9 ESV

You are the God who does miracles;
you have shown people your power.

PSALM 77:14 NCV

The LORD is your keeper;
The LORD is your shade on your right hand.

PSALM 121:5 NASB

This God is our God for ever and ever;
he will be our guide even to the end.

PSALM 48:14 NIV

Because he holds fast to me in love, I will deliver him;
I will protect him, because he knows my name.

PSALM 91:14 ESV

The LORD of Heaven's Armies is here among us;
the God of Israel is our fortress.

PSALM 46:7 NLT

You equipped me with strength for the battle;
you made those who rise against me sink under me.

PSALM 18:39 ESV

Your kingdom is built on what is right and fair.
Love and truth are in all you do.

PSALM 89:14 NCV

The LORD takes delight in his people;
he crowns the humble with victory.

PSALM 149:4 NIV

LORD, you give light to my lamp.
My God brightens the darkness around me.

PSALM 18:28 NCV

He made the moon to mark the seasons;
the sun knows its time for setting.

PSALM 104:19 ESV

The righteous flourish like the palm tree
and grow like a cedar in Lebanon.

PSALM 92:12 ESV

It is you, a person like me,
my companion and good friend.

PSALM 55:13 NCV

I run in the path of your commands,
for you have broadened my understanding.

PSALM 119:32 NIV

God protects me like a shield;
he saves those whose hearts are right.

How joyful are those who fear the LORD—
all who follow his ways!

PSALM 128:1 NLT

Praise the LORD, for the LORD is good;
celebrate his lovely name with music.

PSALM 135:3 NLT

In God, whose word I praise—
in God I trust and am not afraid.

PSALM 56:4 NIV

_____

_____

_____

_____

_____

_____

_____

_____

_____

_____

_____

_____

_____

_____

_____

_____

_____

_____

_____

Even in darkness light dawns for the upright,
for those who are gracious and compassionate and righteous.

PSALM 112:4 NIV

Let integrity and uprightness preserve me,
for I wait for You.

PSALM 25:21 NASB

The humble will see their God at work and be glad.
Let all who seek God's help be encouraged.

PSALM 69:32 NLT

Let me hear of your unfailing love each morning,
for I am trusting you.

PSALM 143:8 NLT

Keep me as the apple of your eye;
hide me in the shadow of your wings.

PSALM 17:8 ESV

Teach me your way, LORD, that I may rely on your faithfulness;
give me an undivided heart, that I may fear your name.

PSALM 86:11 NIV

May he give you the desire of your heart
and make all your plans succeed.

PSALM 20:4 NIV

The LORD merely spoke, and the heavens were created.
He breathed the word, and all the stars were born.

PSALM 33:6 NLT

You will show me the path of life;
in your presence is fullness of joy.

PSALM 16:11 NKJV

Your faithfulness flows from one generation to the next;
all that you have created sits firmly in place to testify of you.

PSALM 119:90 TPT

The LORD is compassionate and gracious,
slow to anger and abounding in lovingkindness.

PSALM 103:8, NASB

The LORD is all I need.
He takes care of me.

PSALM 16:5 NCV

Those who love your instructions
have great peace and do not stumble.

PSALM 119:165 NLT

Your promise revives me;
it comforts me in all my troubles.

PSALM 119:50 NLT

O LORD, you are so good, so ready to forgive,
so full of unfailing love for all who ask for your help.

PSALM 86:5 NLT

I have set the LORD always before me;
because he is at my right hand, I shall not be shaken.

PSALM 16:8 ESV

Even when I walk through the darkest valley, I will not be afraid,
for you are close beside me.

Surely your goodness and love will follow me
all the days of my life.

PSALM 23:6 NIV